Releasing

the

Entrepreneurial

Woman

7 Keys of a
Queen

By Michelle Gines

Published by Purpose Publishing

1503 Main Street #168 ✏ Grandview, Missouri

www.purposepublishing.com

ISBN: 978-0-9828379-3-1

Cover design by: Sharon Dailey

Editing by:
Linda Collins, Brenda Cotton, & Rae Lewis

Printed in the United States of America

This book is available at quantity discounts for
bulk purchases. Inquiries may be addressed to:
www.MICHELLEGINES.com

Scriptures referenced in this book are from the King James
Version, New American Standard Version and New
International Versions.

7 Keys of a Queen

Releasing the Entrepreneurial Woman

By Michelle Gines

To God, my first 'true love' and encourager.
I am forever grateful, blessed and fortunate to know you.

To my mother, Sharon Graham, for allowing me to be me-
all the days of my life. Your encouraging spirit is with me daily.

To my children, Zerryn, Brielle & Charis.
Thank you for sharing mommy with the world.
I'm so proud of all of you. You are my legacy.

To my husband, Brian, the love of my life.
Thank you for everything.

contents

foreword by

Pastor Lisa Wesley

I have always believed that every person has creative abilities inside of them. Since we have been created in the image and likeness of God who is the Creator of all things, God has divinely bestowed this creative power upon us.

Each of us also have the capacity to be an entrepreneur. When God put man in the garden and said, *"Dress it and keep it"* (Gen. 2:15), He gave man the power of attorney to conduct His business here on earth. He made us to be stewards over His property, and with that stewardship accompanies everything we need to handle our business. We may lack the understanding and skills to pursue a business, but the power to do it lies within us. All we need to do is tap the resources.

Michelle has unlocked the mystery and given us the keys to help us get started in her book, *"7 Keys of a Queen: Releasing the Entrepreneurial Woman."* She has given us the resources and the principles we need. Whether you are a man or a woman, this book is a must-have for all who want to begin a business, or have started one.

This book is informational, but it is also Michelle's life. My husband and I have been her Pastors for over ten years, and I can say that Michelle lives the life she preaches. The principles that are outlines in this book have been applied in her own business as well as in her membership in the church. She is full of life and has a passion to help people reach their full potential in Christ. She has a wealth of wisdom and knowledge concerning marketing skills and shares with anyone who will listen.

After reading this book, I have gained more insight and have been challenged in some areas of the business side of pastoring a church. As you read through the *7 Keys of a Queen*, you will be inspired as well as challenged in not only your business, but in your spiritual walk as well. Her keen insight into the Queen of Sheba will enlighten your eyes as to how to conduct your business and how to relate to people in a better way. It will impart a *"spirit of excellence"* in you. Apply the principles found in this book because they have been borne out of the heart of the greatest Businessman on Earth, God our Creator. *"And as He is, so are we hear in the earth."*

Pastor Lisa Wesley
Serves as Co-Pastor with her husband, Apostle Keith Wesley at New Life in Christ International Ministries- Grandview, MO
Co-Author, Marital Fitness…2 Fit 2 Quit

preface

The Queen of Sheba makes a dramatic entrance in 1 Kings 10 and seems to vanish thereafter. Yet her story resonated so with me that I could not, not write this book. I want to share with you, the 7 key things that I learned during this study - things that have literally broke the back of the enemy in my life pertaining to pursuing business.

By the inspiration of God, I've taken the 7 key characteristics of The Queen of Sheba to mobilize and motivate every other *"Business Queen"* in the church and in the world. The women who are wondering whether or not she could be a success or if she should even try. I encourage you to take this journey with me give your all, expand your faith and see where God will guide you.

As we get started know that any road untraveled will be filled with brush, sticks, thorns and debris. However, there have been others that have trod this path and for *your* sake, have left behind nuggets of wisdom that are far greater than just material goods.

The Queen of Sheba, an iconic type of woman in her own right, shares with us some very interesting and necessary keys. I believe you will find all 7 most helpful in launching and/or maintaining an entrepreneurial path.

It doesn't matter if your business has not been launched or if you're considering expanding. When you look at the gifts the Queen possessed and cultivated, you will find they are absolutely essential; even now, over 3,200 years later. It just goes to show that wisdom *is* the stability of the times.

> *And I will give unto thee **the keys of the kingdom of heaven:** and whatsoever thou shalt bind on earth shall be bound in heaven: and whatsoever thou shalt loose on earth shall be loosed in heaven.*
>
> ***Matthew 16:19***

introduction

The Bible speaks briefly about the Queen of Sheba, but of what is spoken in 1 Kings and 2 Chronicles, she is long remembered beyond her time. So, let's take a little time as we begin to gain a full understanding of what the Queen of Sheba was made of and what her "Queendom" entailed.

The country of Sheba whose name means "Host of Heaven and Peace" was one known for its fragrant perfumes and spices. So, it isn't hard to recognize that a lady of this magnitude, would emerge from such a land. Sheba was made up of about 483,000 square miles of mountains, valley and desert in the present day area of Yemen. Sheba was nestled in the southwestern tip ofArabia, bordering the Red Sea. Further, historians claim that Ethiopia on the western end of the Red Sea, was also a part of Sheba's territory.

Sheba was a wealthy country, advanced in irrigation techniques and hydraulic power. Its people, the Sabeans, built dams as high as 60feet and large earthen wells which contributed to their thriving agriculture and beautiful gardens. Sheba was an area also known for its commodity trading like gold, frankincense and myrrh to kingdoms in India, the Mediterranean and Africa.

The spices of Sheba were highly prized. Frankincense was given as an antidote for poison, and as a cure for chest pains, hemorrhoids and paralysis. Myrrh, an ingredient in fragrant oils and cosmetics, was used in preparing bodies for burial, for healing ear, eye and nose ailments and inducing menstruation. Other Sabean spices were saffron, cumin, aloes and galbanum. It appeared to me that the Queen of Sheba was among the first in leading the cosmetic or pharmaceutical industries.

The Queen of Sheba stands today immortalized as an exotic and mysterious woman of power. Born 1020 B.C, her birthplace is said to be Ophir (now Yemen) and that she was educated in Ethiopia. Upon the death of her father in 1005 B.C., Sheba became Queen at the age of fifteen. She is best known as: the wealthy Queen who tested King Solomon.

Sheba was said to be beautiful, intelligent, understanding, resourceful and adventurous. A gracious Queen, she had a melodious voice and was an eloquent speaker. Excelling in public relations and international diplomacy, she was also a competent ruler. It is from her that we can all learn.

The Journey of the Female Entrepreneur

Now, word had gotten back to the Queen regarding King Solomon, who was the son of David and Bathsheba. At the birth of Solomon, he was named by the prophet Nathan, Jedidiah, which meant *"Beloved of the Lord"*. It was told that he was the wisest man on the earth. Rumor had come before about his wisdom in discerning of two women and a child; of his fabulous temple, furnishings, men and servants. As well, she knew that he would be wise in even the trade with which she was ruler and maintained watch (her business).

The Queen of Sheba is the first female entrepreneur that is identified in the Bible. There were many great women in the Word, but she stands out for purposes of training the women of God as they pursue the entrepreneurial Spirit within; which God himself bestows upon some.

So, here she was having heard of the great Solomon and his wisdom; she knew that she must meet him, learn from him, share with him and glean. Her story sheds light on a very interesting story that sets the tone for the adventure that we will embark upon in this book.

The Queen of Sheba was endowed with many character qualities and gifts that even the meekest of women possess today. The gifts (skills, talents and abilities) may be lying dormant within or on display in boardrooms across America. Nevertheless, we can learn so much from our sister from years past. Let us see how we can activate, educate and motivate those things within ourselves and like her, leave a legacy.

The meeting of the Queen of Sheba and King Solomon of Israel had significance upon the fate of Israel and the matriarchy of Sheba. It has inspired many of us to write, but for sake of this book and its' story we are going to focus our attention on these *seven* keys that made her legendary.

- **Wisdom**

- **The C-Factor**

- **Principle**

- **Order**

- **Praise**

- **Giving**

- **Legacy**

chapter one

WISDOM
She sought wisdom.

1 Kings 10:1 Now when the Queen of Sheba heard about the fame of Solomon concerning the name of the Lord, she came to test him with hard questions.

Power and riches could not satisfy Sheba's soul, for she possessed an ardent hunger for truth and wisdom. Before her visit to Solomon, she says to her people:

"I desire wisdom and my heart seeketh to find understanding. I am smitten with the love of wisdom.... for wisdom is far better than treasure of gold and silver... It is sweeter than honey, and it maketh one to rejoice more than wine, and it illumineth more than the sun.... It is a source of joy for the heart, and a bright and shining light for the eyes, and a giver of speed to the feet, and a shield for the breast, and a helmet for the head... It makes the ears to hear and hearts to understand."

"...And as for a kingdom, it cannot stand without wisdom, and riches cannot be preserved without wisdom.... He who heapeth up gold and silver doeth so to no profit without wisdom, but he who heapeth up wisdom - no man can filch it from his heart... I will follow the footprints of wisdom and she shall protect me forever. I will seek asylum with her, and she shall be unto me power and strength."

"Let us seek her, and we shall find her; let us love her, and she will not withdraw herself from us, let us pursue her, and we shall overtake her; let us ask, and we shall receive; and let us turn our hearts to her so that we may never forget her." [i]

We are taught in all things that we will need to build on a strong foundation; our home, our children and for oneself. Well, wisdom is a great foundation to build upon.

Sheba "heard" about the wisdom of King Solomon and it compelled her to take the journey of a lifetime to seek it out. I will tell you that women seek all kinds of things: clothing sales, discount malls, spectacular shoes, etc. But it would be wise for each of us to seek *wisdom* with the same zeal, diligence and seriousness- we do for temporal things. It will be required to get started. Any woman desiring to embark upon starting a new business, it would serve her well to do the research. The Queen took it upon herself to go and find out if what she had heard was true. We can learn from Sheba as she took off to find the answers to her hard questions.

I believe that in her search lies two critical character qualities we should cultivate and emulate; ***seeking and asking.***

Seeking

She went to where she could find the answers. She knew Solomon was the wisest man in the land. Now, in the times we live in there may be no one Solomon, but we can find the answers to nearly anything we need to know. It's going to be very important for one just starting out, to do a little due diligence. And due diligence, is the research.

What kind of business are you planning to start? Is it current business expanding or contracting? Is it something you've done before? Have you ever been paid for these services? What will it cost you to get started? What are your chances of survival?

These are **some** of the questions that you will want to know the answer to before investing or jumping in head first. It's important to be savvy in getting the answers to all the questions. As this is part of laying a very strong foundation which is critical to long term existence. Now research will help you with one part of the foundation, there is yet another quality that will also help ensure success.

Asking

There is much that must be done in order to get started, but cannot be accomplished without some asking.

Asking is an area where most people fall by the wayside. You *have to be willing* to ask. In my days of sales and fundraising, I found out that the sooner I "asked" what I really wanted to know, the sooner I'd get the answer I needed to move on to the next step. Even a "No", was better than barking up the wrong tree for too long. If it was the wrong time or if there was not a possibility of actually getting a "Yes" , a "No" answer served me just as well. I also discovered that because time is always of the essence, "hem-hawing around" never works, for me or anyone else. Without a doubt, there will be some things you will just have to flat out ask for when starting your business. Things such as:

Can you help me? Would you be interested in investing? Is this the right location? What would you

17

suggest? Am I going about this the right way? Is there a better way to accomplish this? Who should I contact?

It appears that with the increase of information on the internet and other resources, people have gotten out of the habit of talking directly to people. We are steadily losing our ability to communicate with others. As much as we profess that communication is critical. I would encourage you to put off this habit. It will be imperative for a successful woman to get away from being behind the computer through email, social media and even texting.

Let's face it, most of us at some point in time or another have been disappointed or unimpressed by what I have found behind "the voice", be it the "Charlie" on the popular 1980's television program, "Charlie's Angels", or the "Wizard" at the end of the yellow brick and mystical road to the land of Oz. Raise your hand if you have ever been disappointed by the actual product when the commercial promised us perfection? The truth is the real answers come by asking the right questions of the right **people** who actually know the **answers**. And believe it or not, most people will share with you, and do so liberally! Some of the most successful people I know, have made the lion's share of their riches, by sharing the knowledge that was given to them or they acquired. You will also find that successful people often have mentors. The mentors share with them what to do and what not to do; minimizing pitfalls and failures. Seriously, no matter what you're trying to do, there will always be someone who has been there and done that.

Wisdom Will Require a "Mental Ascent"

Success is not purely mental; but the art of changing our thinking begins with changing your mind. A few key

18

principles can make a difference in the way successful women view the world and handle the challenges that may come their way:

℘ Practice optimism
Sheba came with an expectation that if this man was so wise; he could answer all of her questions.

℘ Get out of your comfort zone
Sheba left the comfort of her own home taking an arduous 1500 mile journey seeking wisdom. You won't find the answers unless you go.

℘ Use the power of belief to create success
Sheba believed that what she wanted (wisdom) would be found.

℘ Choose to deal with your circumstances
Only you can change them - even if it's just the way you think about them.

℘ Be mindful of the real importance of flexibility
Instead of seeing walls and hurdles, see windows of opportunity and avenues to success.

Now, getting started does require a little more than we may have bargained for. I'm sure as Sheba ventured out, there were probably some times on the back of that camel that she even asked, *"What am I doing?"*. However, I'm also sure her conclusion was, *"once I get there and ask him, I will know what I need to do to be better"*. Those kind of times will come for you as well. It will be well worth it in the end. As with our exercise and diet, they say, *"no pain no gain"*. We have to put in the work to get the results we really want and that's just as true in business.

Here is a good model for long-range planning that's an organized, multi-step process that helps you create a business road map.

It will enable you to anticipate the future and address key issues before they become crises or missed opportunities. Long-range planning is a process of decisions:

Where am I now?	$\Rightarrow$	*Present*
Where do I want to go?	$\Rightarrow$	*Future*
How will I get there?	$\Rightarrow$	*Road Map*
When?	$\Rightarrow$	*Time frame*
With whom?	$\Rightarrow$	*Human Capital*
How to get organized?	$\Rightarrow$	*Structure*
What are the costs?	$\Rightarrow$	*Financial*
What are the benefits?	$\Rightarrow$	*Upside*
What are the risks?	$\Rightarrow$	*Downside*

So, start by analyzing the external environment - economic, political, demographic, social and technological. Surely Sheba must have considered these things and made decisions considering all these factors. In the end, she still had to keep good watch over her country (her business) even in her absence.

Now, appraise your company's resources and capabilities; it's human capital - physical and financial, plus intangible assets like good will, service and quality. All of these things contribute to the overall health of your business.

As well, you will want to analyze your company's strengths and weaknesses compared to competitors. Do you know what will make you different from your competitors?

If your business is already started, ask yourself: Am I better or worse than my competitors? What is your value proposition?

It's important to answer these questions going in, as once you're in the throes of running the business, it gets difficult to go back and get the foundation in order. We want to do that early on.

So, here's a novel idea: identify marketplace voids, opportunities, niches and crucial success factors. Ideas are a dime a dozen, but solutions are priceless. I heard a speaker say: focus on finding solutions to migraines, not headaches. With this in mind, it'll make it easier for you to find out what kind of business to start. Once you've identified a place you can start and maintain, you will find your sweet spot. This often includes pricing, value and convenience, but could also include rate of return, time savings and limited risk.

Therefore whosoever heareth these sayings of mine, and doeth them, I will liken him unto a wise man, which built his house upon a rock:[25] And the rain descended, and the floods came, and the winds blew, and beat upon that house; and it fell not: for it was founded upon a rock. Matthew 7:24-25 KJV

The foundation of any business is best set by tilling the ground, discovering what's underneath and then building. A foundation set upon a rock can weather many storms. Use the tools I've shared here as a starting ground and remember to create a plan, execute and re-evaluate regularly. This will offer you great stability in the long run.

Know When You Need Help & Ask For It.

Successful women entrepreneurs not only understand the value of asking for help; they also know when to ask. Feeling that you have to struggle heroically on your own will not lead to the kind of success that women all over the world have achieved. Remember, asking for help at a crucial point is not about just responding to crisis. Successful women plan ahead and think strategically, asking themselves, *"What kind of help will I need?" "When will it be most effective?"* That help can come in a variety of ways, i.e.; getting help from family and friends, forming a partnership with a manufacturer or finding a distributor to take the load off of you. You just have to know that there is help out there when you need it and ask for it. Don't be fearful.

Sheba shared her heart with Solomon. I'm sure she asked about business things as well as about personal things. Either way, she knew what she needed and was willing to ask for it. She got the support she needed and so will you.

chapter two

THE C-FACTOR
Sheba had Confidence, Comrades & Confidantes

1 Kings 10:2 ***And she came to Jerusalem with a very great train, with camels that bare spices, and very much gold, and precious stones: and when she was come to Solomon, she communed with him of all that was in her heart.***

How did the Queen of Sheba learn of King Solomon's wisdom? The leader of her trade caravans, Tamrin, owned 73 ships and 787 camels, mules and asses, with which he journeyed as far as India. Having also traded with Israel, he brought gold, ebony and sapphires to Solomon, for use by his 700 carpenters and 800 masons who were building the great temple of Jerusalem. Let's take a listen in to what he shared.

Tamrin *told Sheba about the temple and how Solomon administered just judgment, and how he spake with authority, and how he decided rightly in all matters which he enquired into, and how he returned soft and gracious answers, and how there was nothing false about him. Each morning, Tamrin related to the Queen about all the wisdom of Solomon, how he administered judgment ... and how he made feasts, and how he taught wisdom, and how he directed his servants and all his affairs... and how no man defrauded another... for in his wisdom he knew those who had done wrong, and he chastised them, and made them afraid, and they did not repeat their evil deeds, but they lived in a state of peace.*

"And the Queen was struck dumb with wonder at the things that she heard... and she thought in her heart that she would go to him; and she wept by reason of the greatness of her pleasure in those things that Tamrin had told her.... When she pondered upon the long journey she thought that it was too far and too difficult to undertake. But she became very wishful and most desirous to go that she might hear his wisdom, and see his face, and embrace him, and petition his royalty." [ii]

Here we identify yet another character quality of the Queen. She surrounded herself with people she could put her confidence in and she herself was also confident. It's interesting that there was at least one and probably many others, with kingdoms as well, in her camp. They told her about the wisdom, grandeur and splendor of the King. It's very important as a woman in business to be able to have the "right" kind of people in your camp. The ability to be confident in oneself is among the chief qualities to develop.

Confidence

"When this Queen heard of the virtue and prudence of Solomon, she had a great mind to see him...she being desirous to be satisfied by her own experience, and not by a bare hearing (for reports thus heard are likely enough to comply with a false opinion); she resolved to come to him, in order to have a trial of his wisdom, while she proposed questions of very great difficulty and entreated that he would solve their hidden meaning." [iii]

Sheba's desire to encounter Solomon was fervent enough for her to embark on a 1,500 mile journey, across the desert sands of Arabia, along the coast of the Red Sea, up into Moab, and over the Jordan River to Jerusalem. A journey required at least six months travel time each way, camels could only travel about 20 miles per day.

The Queen of Sheba must have had an inclination in her heart to seek wisdom and with that she added the confidence to take the necessary steps. You will find that as an entrepreneur, you too, will have to be confident within yourself for the journey that lies ahead. We see that Sheba had the wherewithal to get her to the place she needed to go, seek someone who was wise and ask the questions. There are often times in our lives when we don't always feel as though we have all the answers, necessary skills, educational background or aptitude required. It is from within, that we have to gain a healthy perspective of who we are and go on the journey. In that, know that the process will teach some of what we don't know and the remainder will come by faith. You must believe that what we desire, will be ours when it lines up with the will of God for our life.

There are those of us that know, beyond any shadow of a doubt, that God has given us a purpose in this life and the desire for us to fulfill it. There are those who never venture out because of fear of failure, life, family fatigue or just plain ole' being lazy. The truth is, there is something in all of us (and if you're reading this book, there is something in you) saying, *"Yes, I should be doing it"*. If so, then do it!

See Yourself as a Player

Being successful at anything requires that you see yourself as a legitimate player. You are more than entitled to sit at the table, you can start your own table. When you begin, you may not know all the rules of the game or all the other players, but you can learn it all with practice and perseverance.

Take a Calculated First Step

Be willing to take the first step like other women who have found themselves in your same boat. It's no surprise that every successful woman started with a first step in the direction she wanted to go. Taking the first step breaks down fear and inertia and substitutes it with anticipation and excitement and accomplishment. Remember Sheba, no one had to tell her to go; she went. You too will have to go.

I remember a pivotal moment in my life came when I learned that Nike was a Greek word for "victory". My husband and I were studying for a prayer meeting we were asked to speak at and it was part of the lesson we were going to teach. When my eyes and heart (read and understood) that small word 'Nike=Victory' and considered that small word that caused many to sport tennis shoes for fashion – it ignited the passion in me for Christ! I realized that their slogan had led them to victory over and over again. So now, their slogan is now *my* slogan, *"Just do it."* I have found that by just doing it, **it** has brought great victories in my life.

I speak to you not as one who says to do something, but has not done it herself, personally, but as one who says do it and has done it, with victory as my testimony. But I realize that confidence doesn't come easy for one and all; in some cases it has to be mustered up, or affirmed. Today, I share with you. ***Just do it!*** And your victory will be released in the name of confidence.

Comrades

Another piece of the C-Factor I noted in the study of the Queen of Sheba is; she summoned him with all that was in her heart. You know I have found that the human race needs people around us that will tell us the truth, guide us in the way and provide counsel for us businesswomen. It is confidence in knowing that we don't have to go it alone. Proverbs 24:6 tells us *"there is safety in a multitude of counselors"*.

And there is safety to help us make good decisions, steer us away from dangers and pitfalls as well as shepherd us in the way of success. It will be important as a businesswoman to identify those whom you can trust and rely upon. These are the other *vital people* within your circle.

Perseverance, tenacity, and overcoming at all odds were certainly some of Sheba's character traits. As we find with her, you have to surround yourself with people that want to see you succeed. Ones that will share with you and allow you to share with them. I encourage you to persevere in identifying these people that you might rightly entrust them. Have you ever had someone say to you, "You can't see the forest for the trees" or "Its right in front of your face, but you can't see it"? Well if not, consider yourself lucky. The truth is we often miss the jewels in our lives because we have failed to look at them as valuable.

So, make up in your mind today that you will look around, identify the comrades and let them know that they are of value to you and you appreciate what they are to you.

If you look around and find some missing; look again or seek out the type of people you want in this group. Be honest with yourself. You will find that among the group of great ones there will be those that truly are not ones to be trusted. Identifying those that should not be trustworthy is just as important as identifying the ones that are. But when considering the group of people in your comrade zone, start here first.

Refuse to Believe Conventional Wisdom

Conventional wisdom can be helpful, giving us the benefit of others' experience. It can also be a restraint. A chorus of naysayers who believe they know better than you do, may imply that your situation will never change, or that what you want is impossible.

Surrounding yourself with the "right" people and trusting your own intuition will prove to be all you need to keep going forward. Haven't you often heard people say, *"I wish I had followed my first mind?"* Of course you have. We've all heard that and said that. I tell people that your first mind is the Holy Spirit. The more often you follow Him, the more often you will find yourself in the will of God. Who can lose when God is with us?

Get the Support You Need by Asking For It.

Look around and identify Godly mentors and other successful people that will support you. Even the toughest and most tenacious among us needs to feel supported in what they're doing. We all need that occasional verbal pat on the back, *"You can do it; you're on the right track"*, *"Here, let me help you"*. To begin and persist in any adventure, be it career, business or life, we need support. Although we hesitate to ask for it, there is nothing wrong with seeking and finding support. In fact, we often learn so much in the process that we end up succeeding even the more. Of course, getting constructive advice from friends and associates depends both on their intentions and on your ability to receive it in the right frame of mind. Asking for advice or support from people who are reluctant to give it or who do not genuinely have an interest in your success, can sometimes make you feel defensive or belittled. Yet, even then, if you lower your defenses, listen carefully, and ignore what isn't useful, you can still get helpful information.

It Is Imperative to Build Up a Network of Support

See that you have a place where people love you and believe in you and will be honest with you. You can use them as your sounding board. Every successful woman needs a sounding board.

Now if you can't find a support group for your specific field, form your own. You can reach out and get exactly what you need. Companies use a model for developing new programs and projects within their companies and having learned from the best. Here are a few tips:

Contact people who are in the same business or industry as you - call them up and ask for a meeting.

I found that in most every case they will say, "Yes". Most women do not think in terms of *"I can't or won't share"*. On the contrary, in my experience, they were happy to share their manuals, their policies and their procedures. We didn't see each other as competitors.

Host a luncheon or roundtable, meeting every 6-8 weeks with five women from different companies.

By joining a group or creating one, you will find that other women are willing to share experiences and to encourage you. If you haven't been part of a professional group or women's club, you may not fully appreciate the value of having like-minded women surrounding you.

Confidantes

Another point I want to highlight here very quickly is this. Confidantes share some characteristics that will need to be discerned. This group of people is your inner circle and inner circle people are needed more than a whole lot of others.

They are:

- *The people who, when you're with them it's just like being alone because you can be your natural self.*

- *The people who are with you when you're up, when you're down, when you're stuck, when you've been dogged out; they are with you.*

- *The people who live and breathe off of their relationship with you. They need <u>you</u> to nurture the relationship with them.*

- *They care about you. Their commitment is to you, not your cause. They are not overwhelmed by your prestige, your recognition or your monies, but more so because they want success for you as if your success is their own.*

*℘ **The ones you can trust to tell you the truth, and to whom you can divulge your secret faults; you can trust them with your life.***

Everyone, in fact most people, will not fall into this group. However, the ones who do, are special. You have to treat them special.

Sometimes people wonder how certain people take up the role of armor bearer or best friend. We kid with each other about being our BFF (Best Friend Forever), but the truth is, we all need some real BFF's. Business has ups and downs, valleys and peaks and you will always need someone to share all of it with you. Recognize these people and keep them close to your heart.

Over the course of a lifetime, you will be blessed to have had three real confidantes. These are the people you could never pay to do what they do, but without them you could never do all that you do.

chapter three

THE PRINCIPLES & THE PROMISES
Sheba's heart felt, what her eyes beheld..

*I Kings 10: 3-5 And Solomon told her all her questions: there was not anything hid from the king, which he told her not. **⁴And when the Queen of Sheba had seen all Solomon's wisdom, and the house that he had built, ⁵And the meat of his table, and the sitting of his servants, and the attendance of his ministers, and their apparel, and his cupbearers, and his ascent by which he went up unto the house of the LORD; there was no more spirit in her.*

> *"If you have integrity, nothing else matters. If you don't have integrity, nothing else matters."*
> -- Alan K. Simpson

We find that as Sheba came unto the King with tough questions, he answered her and withheld not anything from her. He was able to give her an account of everything she had asked. As a woman, I believe the Queen discerned from Solomon that it is very important to be of high regard and standards. One must have a full understanding of who they are and what they stand for in business. We have often heard the phrase, *"If you don't stand for something you will fall for anything"*. I believe that Sheba was quite complete in her questions as she could easily see that he was able to provide an account or an answer to her. People will come to you as a business owner wanting to know how you do business, how do you handle customers, or what are your principles. Even if they don't ask, you'd better believe they are discovering by the way you do business. It would behoove you to consider these things as you plan to venture out or sharpen what's already been started. A good place to start, (and that I share with women all over the country) is to have some guidelines that you live by in all business. Your business should have heart.

Guiding Principles + God's Promises= Engineered Success

It is entirely possible to engineer your own success if you work hard enough at it. It is also possible to engineer the success of your business by instituting sound business principles and by applying them to your business daily. As you build the foundation, you will need to establish ground rules, or guiding principles that you will abide by, and that your employees will abide by. These ground rules will dictate how your business operates, what decisions your business makes, and how other people and other businesses view your business. If you establish these principles up front, there will not be any questions about how you, your employees, or how your business will respond in difficult situations. Success engineering requires a business owner to do a few things:

First, you must decide on your guiding principles based on what you would like the future of your business to look like. If you want your business to have a youthful feel and appeal to a younger generation, then your guiding principles should stipulate that. If your future business is very professional and white collar, then you should include those ideals in your principles so there is no question as to how your business should operate.

34

Second, you will need to hire employees and contractors who agree to abide by your guiding principles. Much like a standard of behavior that larger corporations institute through their human resources office, your guiding principles must be accepted by all of the employees at your company. If even one employee breaks the mold and does not agree with your guiding principles, he or she could create a slippery slope of dissent that will result in your business being undermined. These guiding principles should be put into place and should be adhered to by anyone who wishes to have a future at your company.

Finally, your success engineering should begin with an introspective look at what your guiding principles mean to you and if you as the business leader can uphold them. Principles can make or break a business but if your life reflects your business principles, then they will simply be an extension of who you are, rather than an alter ego that you slip into when you go to work each day. Your guiding principles should be stated clearly and in plain view of your employees and your customers so they all know what you and your business stands for.

Another important attribute for small business success is the distinguishing quality of practicing admirable business ethics. Business ethics, practiced throughout the deepest layers of a company, become the heart and soul of the company's culture and can mean the difference between success and failure. I worked for Hallmark Cards for ten years and I remember there slogan, "When you care enough to send the very best; send a Hallmark." Hallmark is a family company and it came through in their mission and values clearly. It drove how the company operated. The mission and vision of any company must be developed intentionally; your company included.

Benefits of Practicing Business Ethics

In the research study, *"Does Business Ethics Pay?"* by The Institute of Business Ethics (IBE), it was found that companies displaying a *"clear commitment to ethical conduct"* consistently outperform companies that do not display ethical conduct. The Director of IBE, Philippa Foster Black, stated: *"Not only is ethical behavior in business life the right thing to do in principle, we have shown that it pays off in financial returns."* These findings deserve to be considered as an important insight for companies striving for long-term success and growth.

7 Principles of Admirable Business Ethics

1. Be Trustworthy: Recognize customers want to do business with a company they can trust; when trust is at the core of a company, it's easy to recognize. Trust defined, is assured reliance on the character, ability, strength, and truth of a business.

2. Keep an Open Mind: For continuous improvement of a company, the leader of an organization must be open to new ideas. Ask for opinions and feedback from both customers and team members and your company will continue to grow.

3. Meet Obligations: Regardless of the circumstances, do everything in your power to gain the trust of past customers and clients, particularly if something has gone awry. Reclaim any lost business by honoring all commitments and obligations.

4. Have Clear Documents: Re-evaluate all print materials including small business advertising, brochures, and other business documents making sure they are clear, precise and professional. Most important, make sure they do not misrepresent or misinterpret.

5. Become Community-Involved: Remain involved in community-related issues and activities, thereby demonstrating that your business is a responsible community contributor. In other words, stay involved.

6. Maintain Accounting Control: Take a hands-on approach to accounting and record keeping, not only as a means of gaining a better feel for the progress of your company, but as a resource for any "questionable" activities. Gaining control of accounting and record keeping allows you to end any dubious activities promptly.

7. Be Respectful: Treat others with the utmost of respect. Regardless of differences, positions, titles, ages, or other types of distinctions, always treat others with professional respect and courtesy.

Recognizing the significance of business ethics as a tool for achieving your desired outcome is only the beginning. A small business that instills a deep-seated theme of business ethics within its strategies and policies will be evident among customers. Its overall influence will lead to a profitable, successful company.

By recognizing the value of practicing admirable business ethics, and following each of the 7 principles, your success will not be far off.

Let's start by taking a closer look into what the Queen of Sheba saw when she met with King Solomon. Israel during the time of Solomon was a unified kingdom, 30,000 square miles in area - a small but respected power existing peacefully between Assyria and Egypt. Because Solomon

37

was talented in international diplomacy, he negotiated trading agreements with neighboring kings, most notably the Phoenician king, Hiram of Tyre. As a result, his large fleet was built and manned by Phoenicians, and capable of sailing from Esyon-Geber or Eilat on the Red Sea to Ophir, Sheba, and India.

Solomon was (at least initially) a capable administrator, who raised the vast wealth required for his many projects by consolidating his central government and taxing the twelve districts of his kingdom, each which supported his court for one month each year.

Solomon's commitment to building the Temple reflected not only his love of magnificent architecture, but also his piety. Early in his reign, he dedicated himself to God. When God asked him what he most wanted, instead of choosing riches or power, he said, *"Give thy servant therefore an understanding heart to judge Thy people that I may discern between good and evil."* [iv] Pleased at his request, God rewarded him not only with wisdom, but also honor and wealth. *"So King Solomon exceeded all the kings of the earth in riches and in wisdom. And all the earth sought the presence to Solomon, to hear his wisdom, which God had put in his heart."* [v]

Although impressed by Solomon's wealth, Sheba was more interested in his wisdom. Some scholars suggest that her visit was also economically and politically motivated, *"the conclusion of a trade agreement governing both land and sea routes, rather than a meeting of mutual admiration.*[vi]

But imagine if you will, seeing the vastness of his estate and staff and having to govern it all. Good governance starts with a good guiding principle. It would take a special "one" that could orchestrate and articulate the desires that set the hands to the plow to get things moving and kept in order. Business ethics and governing principles will always help you maintain a high standard.

From this study, I found that throughout the ages, many have speculated on the nature of their discussions. They believed they discussed things such as, peace and war, the meaning of life, evil, secrets of death and immortality, the relationship between spirit and body, sexuality, male/female differences, the role of women, the reliability of paternity as a basis for an economic system, the cycles of the moon and tides, and the name and nature of God. But whatever their discussions, most all sources I researched refer to lengthy dialogue occurring between Solomon and the Queen of Sheba.

I imagine she asked about selecting people, making agreements, negotiation - all things women in business would want to know. But my firm belief is that the things he told her, she *did*. I'm sure she went back to her country and established some things, changed others or discarded even others. But all in all, she saw what an efficiently ran business (kingdom) looked like. We too, must learn and glean. The main idea here is realizing that good business ethics and guiding principles are paramount to doing business in the 21st century. It will make the business outlast even the owner. All in all, if you stick with God in the principles; he will show up for you in the promises.

chapter four

ORDER: THE HEART OF YOUR BUSINESS
Sheba saw order, order my steps.

I kings 10:6And she said to the king, It was a true report that I heard in mine own land of thy acts and of thy wisdom. 7Howbeit I believed not the words, until I came, and mine eyes had seen it: and, behold, the half was not told me: thy wisdom and prosperity exceedeth the fame which I heard.

Here's my take on what the Queen of Sheba, in essence said to King Solomon, *"You're awesome! I couldn't believe it until I saw it with my own eyes, but you have made a believer out of me."* I equate this to her not finding anything out of order. Solomon had everything decent and in order. What does that mean to you reading this book? It means, get your stuff in order.

When I say "stuff" I'm referring to things like:

Business Plan	Financials
Business Entity	Marketing Plan
Business Taxes	Insurance
Contracts/ Agreements	Vendors/ Partners

I imagine the Queen of Sheba was on top of all the matters concerning her country (her business) and you should be also. The way to know if you're ready to be an entrepreneur is to make sure you can provide thorough and compelling answers to some very basic questions.

What do you want to build, produce, or provide? For whom? You need to be as specific as possible. (i.e.; what type of consumer are you aiming for? What characteristics do they share? Where do they live?) At the same time, you need to make sure your market is truly large enough, especially if you want to build a scalable business.

Focus on a market or segment that's too limited, and your business by definition will be equally constrained. Also, consider that if the market around you is large and growing, you will have more of a margin for error—time to recoup or re-address the target and a greater chance of success. You should also be able to identify a "pain" that your product or service will alleviate. There's truth in the old expression that people will pay more for a pain reliever than for a vitamin.

> *You should also be able to identify a "pain" that your product or service will alleviate. There's truth in the old expression that people will pay more for a pain reliever than for a vitamin.*

Know Thyself

Another key question to ask yourself is, *"Why am I eager to start this business?"* This is a question that relates both to the market and to you personally.

You need to be able to answer why you believe there's a need for your product or service, why it's superior to anything else available today, and why you will continue to have a competitive advantage?

Just as important, you also need to know why you want to do this personally. Why are you motivated to start this business? How deep is your passion for it? How far are you willing to go to make it a success? The answer to this part of the "why" question needs to satisfy you fully. You need to be totally convinced that you will succeed. Once you make the commitment, and when investors, friends, and family understand that you're driven to achieve your goal, you will find people when and where you least expect, willing to assist. This leads to the following question: how will you build your product or service? This is the essence of the business plan and operating plan. Do not forget to be able to show exactly how you will get it to market. Often, people nail the first part of this question. For example, they have a new patentable approach for mobile search algorithms, a great development team, and a solid timeline. But they often wrongly assume that if they build it, customers will come.

That's simply not the case. It's critical to think through your "go-to-market" strategy. What sales methods, approaches, and channels will you use? What are your creative marketing approaches? Do you have alliances you can form with major companies? Do you have targeted strategic buyers? Have you tested your idea with at least 50 key potential buyers?

There is, of course, the "who" question: "Who's on your team?" Take a hard look at your own skill set. What are your strengths, and what kind of talent would complement your background? Who can you attract to your team? Who will serve on your advisory board? Who will attract investors? Is this a business that you want to build and run? Or would you consider hiring a CEO at some point along the way? Is this a "lifestyle" business, or are you ready to scale your idea into the next billion dollar company? These are the critical questions.

Winning Qualities

Answering these questions is what forms the basis of your business plan—a living document that morphs every few months but nonetheless is a foundation upon which you build. The days of five-year business plans are long gone; but having a clear crisp five-year vision, and then a solid 12-to-18 month operating plan, will keep you in good stead. There are many resources with templates for good business plans. You will find great tools and resources in the Business Treasure Chest section of this book. Overall, keeping it simple is my motto along with keeping it flexible.

If you're ready to think big, its worth looking into the research of Daida Thomson, a colleague who decided not to take the entrepreneurial plunge right away. Instead, she decided to find out just what are the attributes of successful ventures. She lists seven criteria that almost all companies share that not only hit $100 million in annual sales but grow exponentially and hit the $1 billion mark. There's sound advice here even for the company still in incubation.

So hold fast to your vision, but develop a plan, and begin with the end in mind. We will discuss this in further detail a little later on in the book.

Strengthen Your Business Acumen

Now, in addition to what you're going to need to develop some if you don't already have it. What is Business acumen, you ask? Business acumen is an almost intuitive and applicable understanding of *how* your company makes money. It includes a thorough understanding of what drives profitability and cash flow, a market focused approach to the business, and an overall big picture understanding of the business and its interrelationships with vendors and customers.

Every day, entrepreneurs make crucial decisions that directly affect the overall financial performance of their company. They are challenged with ever-increasing responsibility and accountability for financial, strategic and operational decisions. They must possess the confidence and business acumen to make decisions that build shareholder value and support the organization's overall strategy.

Business acumen is not a technical skill rather it is a set of behaviors that are independent from intelligence, technical skills and financial knowledge. I would imagine the Queen of Sheba didn't have to take a class on building business acumen, but I'd venture to guess that she had internal wherewithal to get what she needed and so should you. So we don't get into a myriad of technical business jargon, here it is - plain and simple.

The following are some tips on how to develop and demonstrate business acumen skills:

People demonstrate business acumen skills by:

- Understanding how the various parts of the business work together to provide value to the customer.
- Consistently selecting the best course of action when making business decisions.
- Minimizing risks to the organization in the decisions they make.
- Applying financial savvy and analytical thinking to the decision process.

People can develop a business acumen mindset when they are making decisions by applying the following five simple steps:

1. **Reflect before Deciding** – Stop and think, reflect on your experiences of what worked in the past.

2. **Analyze** – Gather quantitative and qualitative data before you evaluate and draw conclusions.

3. **Create** – Be creative when solving problems, don't go for the obvious answers. Instead, look for unique solutions that will add value.

4. **Collaborate with Others to Get Things Done** – Know who to get on your side and use their talents too!

5. **Take Action** – Get things moving while showing agility and perseverance to complete the task.

As we close this chapter, let's understand the key thing. Getting and keeping your business in order will prove invaluable in the years ahead. Think of it this way; if you were gone tomorrow-could someone pick up and run your business or will it close because the owner in no longer there? A business kept decently and in order will live long past the original owner.

chapter five

EVERY BUSINESS NEEDS PRAISE
Praise Sheba, Sheba praised.

*¹ Kings 10:8**Happy are thy men, happy are these thy servants, which stand continually before thee, and that hear thy wisdom. ⁹Blessed be the LORD thy God, which delighted in thee, to set thee on the throne of Israel: because the LORD loved Israel for ever, therefore made he thee king, to do judgment and justice.***

During Sheba's six month-long visit with Solomon, she conversed with him daily. The **Kebra Negast** informs us that *"the Queen used to go to Solomon and return continually, and hearken unto his wisdom, and keep it in her heart. And Solomon used to go and visit her, and answer all the questions which she put to him... and he informed her concerning every matter that she wished to enquire about."* [vii] Frequently, they roamed Jerusalem together, as she questioned him and watched him at work.

Once, observing a laborer wearing ragged garments, sweating, carrying a stone on his head and a jug of water around his neck, Solomon mused:

"Look at this man. Wherein am I superior to this man? In what am I better than this man? Wherein shall I glory over this man? For I am a man and dust and ashes, who tomorrow will become worms and corruption, and yet at this moment I appear like one who will never die. As is his death, so is my death, and as is his life, so is my life.

Then what is the use of us, the children of men, if we do not exercise kindness and love upon earth? Are we not all nothingness, mere grass of the field, which withereth in its season and is burnt in the fire? On the earth we wear costly apparel... we provide ourselves with sweet scents... but even whilst we are alive we are dead in sin and in transgressions. Blessed is the man who knoweth wisdom, compassion and the fear of God." [viii]

Whether Sheba was an adoring adolescent in search of a wise hero, or a confident, powerful young woman who journeyed to Jerusalem to challenge Solomon, she was impressed with his wisdom, compassion, justice and wealth. **I Kings** tells us:

"And when the Queen of Sheba had seen all the wisdom of Solomon, and the house that he had built, and the food of his table, and the attendance of his ministers...she said to the King, `It was a true report that I heard in mine own land of thine acts, and of thy wisdom. Howbeit I believed not the words, until I came, and mine eyes had seen it; thou hast wisdom and prosperity exceeding the fame which I heard. Happy are thy men...that stand continually before thee, and that hear thy wisdom.'" [ix]

Josephus also states that she was surprised to learn that the flattering reports she had heard about Solomon were true, *"that she was amazed at the wisdom of Solomon.... She was in the greatest admiration imaginable, insomuch that she was not able to contain the surprise she was in, but openly confessed how wonderfully she was affected."* [x]

The story of King Solomon and the Queen of Sheba had many interesting nuggets that I found extremely important to the story of who she was. One thing I found in the midst of the scripture is the fact that after she had seen it all and had spent time with him; she praised him and His God. Praise is yet another character quality she shares with every one of us.

In business, it makes sense to give honor where it is due. Often people miss the boat on offering praise, in particular, to people who are closest to them. But we won't be a victim of not giving praise.

Praise God

The Queen of Sheba offered praise to Solomon and His God. I cannot stress enough our need to honor our God from whom all blessings flow. He is the Giver of Life and of ideas, wealth and wisdom. The Word of God tells us *"the beginning of wisdom is the fear of God"*.

"You may say to yourself, "My power and the strength of my hands have produced this wealth for me". But remember the LORD your God, for it is he who gives you the ability to produce wealth, and so confirms his covenant, which he swore to your forefathers, as it is today. If you ever forget the LORD your God and follow other gods and worship and bow down to them, I testify against you today that you will surely be destroyed." (Deuteronomy 8:17-18 NIV).

The LORD, in the verse above says to remember to acknowledge Him as the Source of your success. A lot of people fail to remember the Lord in their times of success and victory. This forgetfulness is extremely fatal. Who gets the credit for your success and blessings? One of the beautiful things in the account of the Queen of Sheba was that she gave praise to God for having been the one to bestow the wisdom and the honor to King Solomon, as well as furnishing the lavishness he enjoyed.

He was so obviously blessed and favored, that she could not help but praise his God because even she understood that a man could not acquire this in and of his own doing, but only by His God.

No matter what lot we find ourselves in life, know one thing for sure, no success you could ever amass could be accomplished by your own hand. Only God gives and in that, He can also take away. Praise God in all things and every chance you get.

Praise Employees

You can tell your colleagues, co-workers and employees how much you value them and their contribution any day of the year. Trust me. No occasion is necessary. In fact, small surprises and tokens of your appreciation, spread throughout the year, help the people in your work life feel valued all year long.

Looking for ideas about how to praise and thank employees? Here are seven ways to show your appreciation to employees and co-workers.

℘ **Praise work done well by saying 'thank you''**
Identify the specific actions that you found admirable. Show your appreciation for their hard work and contributions. And, don't forget to say "please" often as well. Social niceties do belong in business. A more gracious, polite workplace is appreciated by all.

℘ Ask about their life outside of work

Ask about their family, their hobbies, their weekend or a special event they attended. Your genuine interest - as opposed to being nosy – causes people to feel valued and cared about.

℘ Offer flexible scheduling

Especially during the holidays, if feasible. If work coverage is critical, post a calendar so people can balance their time off with that of their co-workers.

℘ Know those that labor among you

Know people well enough to present a small gift occasionally. An appreciated gift, and the gesture of providing it, will brighten up your co-worker's day.

℘ If you can afford to, give staff money

End of the year bonuses, attendance bonuses, quarterly bonuses and gift certificates say "thank you" quite nicely.

℘ Everyone appreciates food

Take co-workers or staff to lunch for a birthday, a special occasion or for no reason at all. Let your guests pick the restaurant.

℘ Provide opportunity

People want chances for training and cross-training. They want to participate on a special committee where their talents are noticed. They like to attend professional association meetings and represent your organization at civic and philanthropic events.

These are some ways to show appreciation to employees and co-workers. Stretch your imagination. There are hundreds of other employee and co-worker appreciation

51

ideas just waiting to be found. They'll bring you success in employee motivation and recognition and in building a positive, productive workplace.

Praise Customers

Great customer relations start with happy employees. Every employee who answers the phone reveals the mood of the company to the person calling. Customer service starts with the internal customer. Creating an atmosphere where listening and being helpful, matters and it will carry over into all aspects of the business; especially customer service.

Great internal communication creates great customer relations. Great communication and respect within a company has a ripple effect. Seeing a team of people work well together has an incredible impact on an organization, starting with employees and emanating out to the customer. That's what makes business successful. It's the focus on the people so that no energy is spent in unproductive activity or thought. That's success and everything else flows as a result of it.

Great company cultures start by modeling the values you espouse. That's all I have to say about that.

Great customer relationships start with treating customers, vendors, and employees with honesty and integrity. Creating an environment that empowers everyone in the company to have a sense of ownership for internal and external customer satisfaction, unleashes creative potential of everyone in the company.

Great feedback will come when you ask for it and use it to create new products or improve existing ones.

Great relationships with your vendors come by safeguarding them much like you do with your staff. Take personal responsibility for mix ups. Don't pass the buck. Take interest and take action.

Great businesswomen go the extra mile and they are willing to invest the extra dollar. Even if it costs you extra money to settle a problem, consider that you're spending money on positive PR. It's money well spent. One unhappy customer tells more people than you can imagine.

Great customers are the ones you know. If you don't meet them in person, get to know them over the phone. Pay attention when they mention events in their stores or stories about their children. Know their payment history and thank them if they keep a good record.

Great companies get people involved in the company. Some businesses invite good customers to sit in on informal board of advisor meetings. Others involve customers in special events, parties, cruises, etc.. Invite customers to join in on the fun.

The Queen of Sheba was great and so was King Solomon. You too can be great in your business. Learn and grow. The success of your business is determined by your happy employees, happy vendors and happy customers.

Be great at keeping people happy!

chapter six

MAKE IT YOUR BUSINESS TO GIVE
She gave and wasn't left empty.

1 Kings 10:10 **And she gave the king an hundred and twenty talents of gold, and of spices very great store, and precious stones: there came no more such abundance of spices as these which the Queen of Sheba gave to king Solomon. ¹¹And the navy also of Hiram, that brought gold from Ophir, brought in from Ophir great plenty of almug trees, and precious stones.**

After she had visited him for six months, she chose to return to her own country. Before she left, she gave Solomon 120 talents of gold (10 million dollars), precious stones and spices in great abundance, and highly prized sandalwood for his temple. In the Biblical story, *"Solomon gave to the Queen of Sheba all her desire, whatsoever she asked...besides that which Solomon gave her of his royal bounty."* [xi]

How nice of the Queen to share with King Solomon out of her abundance! But there was clearly a key quality that we need mention for the entrepreneurs. It was **giving** and a **heart for giving**. I thought it was interesting that when the Queen was preparing for the trip and calling for gifts to present the King, she left no stone unturned. We can learn a lot from a woman like this. First, she came carrying four and one half tons of gold alone. And that was only a portion of what she brought to give to him. I imagine that she didn't want to come before the King with a gift not worthy of him, so she made sure that what she brought would be fitting for the King.

Can you envision the herd of camels bearing gifts? Literally, camel after camel after camel! It must have been something to behold coming into Jerusalem. Her caravan of 797 camels, mules, and asses laden with provisions and gifts for Solomon, carrying anywhere from 200-300 pounds each, would certainly be a spectacle in the days we live in now! You can imagine, she must have had many armed guards to protect her from desert brigands as well as a host of servants. Surely she was known when she came to town.

Now in the times of the Queen, it was customary to bring gifts to a personal meeting. The gift-giving was a way of demonstrating submission to someone who was in a superior position, be it government, religious or military. So she was doing what was customary, but her gesture would also ensure a blessing for herself. This is a way that you too can ensure a blessing to your own business. There is a great Apostle in Atlanta, Georgia by the name of Apostle Skip Horton. Each time he visits our church, he presents our leaders with a gift, and declares three things: *"Wise men still bring gifts"*, *"givers are getters"* and *"givers are gainers"*. I believe that to be true, so much so, I wouldn't exchange this principle for anything in the world. I have found that this key is a mainstay for all entrepreneurs.

Giving

It's important to note that giving isn't always in the form of money. It is giving of oneself, one's time and one's talent. Plan to make a difference. Making a difference doesn't usually happen by accident. You make it happen. Let it not be said that your life was spent idly. Instead, do something for someone else. Here are some examples of giving without money:

 ℘ **Take your daughter or someone else's to work.**
Support national events sponsored by organizations and take your daughter to work day. You don't have to wait until that one day, introduce young people to your business any day.

 ℘ **Engender the Spirit of giving back in others.**
If you are blessed in your life, you need to give back and be a blessing to others. We all have learned much from others and their experiences; we should give back in that same way.

 ℘ **Make people feel good and capable.**
When a person comes forward with a new idea that's a risk, if you say, I think you can do it; they're going to do it.

 ℘ **Grant informational interviews.**
If you are swamped with too many requests, schedule a seminar or an open door day and invite people to come at the same time.

 ℘ **Volunteer your time.**
Help others and help yourself. I've never volunteered with the idea that I would gain something, but inevitably I did every time.

 ℘ **Teach others.**
Make opportunities to teach others by speaking at schools and organizations.

 ℘ **Start a program to help others learn.**
Education is the key to self reliance. A program can work at any level, from local grass roots to national.

A Heart to Give

Each one must do just as he has purposed in his heart, not grudgingly or under compulsion, for God loves a cheerful giver. 2 Corinthians 9:7 NASV

Give generously to him and do so without a grudging heart; then because of this the LORD your God will bless you in all your work and in everything you put your hand to. Deuteronomy 15:10 NIV

The thing we should note in this story is the *heart of a giver*. The Queen was planning the trip and knowing that she was going to meet the wisest King that had ever lived; she must have known in her heart that her questions were going to be satisfied. And she was. And even if she had not, she prepared to give to him out of the abundance of her heart and with cheerfulness. I cannot assure you that for every gift you present to one, you will be presented a gift in return. But I will tell you from my own experience that when I have given out of my heart, in joy and with love, I have received. And many gifts given back to us may not be returned to us in the same manner of substance; but we will experience a return, nonetheless. For a business owner, I would tell you to give, watch and wait as your harvest comes back, year after year.

Now remember that sometimes the harvest will be learning when it's time to pull out or when to expand; it will be having favor with God and man; or having the wherewithal to gain a new contract or opportunity. However it comes back to you in return, be grateful. The heart of a giver is the one that can be cultivated. If you're not there yet, purpose in your heart to get there.

How do I Cultivate a Giving Heart, You Ask?

Get started - No matter whether you earn a lot of money, or **very** little, you should start giving now. Some people decide to wait until they are making a certain amount of money, or reach a certain age. Almost every time, they express regret that they didn't start giving early. You can make a difference by starting to give money away now. Even students living on very limited incomes, benefit by sowing a seed into good ground.

Pick an amount - You should pick an amount that you want to give away. You may want to do this on a weekly basis, or monthly basis. You may choose an annual goal, but if you do, be sure to break it down into monthly targets. It is often easiest to start with a percentage of your income. A good place to start is by giving ten percent of your income. For some, this may seem like a lot, and yet if you set it up as an automatic gift each month you will hardly notice it. And yet, it will be able to make a significant difference in the lives of others. 10% is what God has chosen as the portion we give back to Him. This is essential for local churches to do the work of the ministry and advance the kingdom of God.

Set goals to increase the amount – Once you have chosen how much you will give away to start with, set goals to increase that, over time. You may be giving away ten percent now, but you may have a goal to increase to twenty percent, thirty percent or even more, over time. This increase may take many years to meet, but it can be an important motivator as you work towards bigger life goals.

Be anonymous – In your giving there are really two types of anonymity and both are valuable. One type is where no one knows who it was that gave the money. There is no record of the person giving the money. The only persons that know are you and God. The other type of anonymity is where you know and it is registered that you gave the money, however it is not made public. The benefit of this is that you receive a tax receipt. For example when I give to my church, the gift is recorded and a tax receipt is issued. Only a couple of people involved in the accounting process know about my gift. It is never announced or acknowledged otherwise. If you want, you can turn around and give your tax return away also!

More than money – you don't need to give just money. You can give away **possessions.** This might be giving away used clothes to the Salvation Army or Goodwill. It might mean donating something around the house that you don't use anymore. Someone I know recently donated a drum set that their kids didn't use any more to a church. You can also **donate your time by volunteering.** Look for places to contribute with an investment of your time. This can often be extra rewarding as you are connected directly to the work that is taking place. Giving will do both your heart and your business good. Try it, soon!

> *The government offers tax deductions for charitable donations because it is a practice that they want to encourage. It is **good stewardship** to take advantage of those tax breaks.*

I think it's important to make the point that Sheba gave and wasn't left empty. I promise that the more you give the more you'll gain; in resources, time, opportunities, appreciation, love, joy, esteem and the list goes on and on. I dare you to give and see what *you'll* gain in return.

chapter seven

LEAVE A LEGACY
Let Sheba show you how.

1 Kings 10:12 *And the king made of the almug trees pillars for the house of the LORD, and for the king's house, harps also and psalteries for singers: there came no such almug trees, nor were seen unto this day.* *13And king Solomon gave unto the Queen of Sheba all her desire, whatsoever she asked, beside that which Solomon gave her of his royal bounty. So she turned and went to her own country, she and her servants.*

Driven by Legacy

As part of my philosophy, I believe we should all do the most with what we have been given. Unfortunately, in stark contrast to this belief, most people go to their grave with many of their best works left in them. Rare is the event in which a person gives everything they have to achieve a worthwhile goal. Most people never give their all and as a result, probably left a little too much talent, skill and potential on the proverbial table of life. This chapter is to remind you not to leave your best works undone. Instead, leave behind a legacy.

Focusing on leaving a legacy, ultimately reminds us that life is short. Whether you get 40 years or 95, it is your responsibility to do the most with what you have, and leave this world a better place than you found it. To do this, you need to discover and cultivate your gifts, take care of yourself to ultimately take care of others, and seek to impact as many people as positively as you can. A great goal is to leave this world and the people in it with a little more than when you got here, and never to rest until you have fulfilled that task.

Part of what motivates me every day is *legacy*. I want to leave the world in a much better state than I found it. When my children, grandchildren and others look back over my life, I want them to do so with an understanding that my intent was to leave them a legacy; to live my life in such a way that it can be admired and modeled. I want my students, both adults and children, to be legacy-minded; to consider the generations that come after them. So I ask you: What is your legacy? Let's consider the Queen of Sheba's legacy. It says that she brought and gave to Solomon, a gift of so much almug wood, that they have never seen that much ever again. And though her story is accounted in less than a dozen scriptures, her legacy remains.

I have been told by my different friends that I am an optimist. I think of it more as a pursuit toward excellence. I have also been told that I push people hard to be better, to not accept mediocrity including my own children. I agree, but please know I push myself harder still. Unfortunately, when you live your life thinking about legacy, it tends to ruffle feathers. It is not my intent rather quite the opposite is true.

My understanding lately has me doing some "system thinking" about seeing individuals from a perspective of the way God sees us. A perspective that honors people rather than neutralizes them (gender, race, circumstance, spirituality, physical presence, and professional well-being) is important as a business owner. Will this business just be in existence for my lifetime or am I building something that will succeed me? When I stand before God and give an account, what will be said of me, how I lived my life, how I loved my family/friends and how I ran my business? I believe that each of these things is important.

Every one of us is going to leave a legacy. It just depends on what kind. What kind of legacy do you want to leave? I encourage you to think about it because knowing how you want to be remembered helps you decide how to live and work every day.

Consider four ways to leave a legacy and identify other legacies you can share.

1. A Legacy of Excellence - Saint Francis of Assisi said, *"It's no use walking anywhere to preach unless your preaching is your walking."* To leave a legacy of excellence, strive to be your best every day. As you strive for excellence, you inspire excellence in others. You serve as a role model for your children, your friends and your colleagues. One person in pursuit of excellence raises the standards and behaviors of everyone around them. Your life is your greatest legacy and since you only have one life to live, live it well and with excellence.

2. A Legacy of Encouragement - You have a choice. You can lift others up or bring them down. Twenty years from now when people think of you what do you want them to remember? The way you encouraged them or discouraged them? I recently spent a day with Ken Blanchard, author of *"The One Minute Manager"*, and I had the opportunity to see so many thank him for his support, encouragement and the difference he has made in my life and many others.

He not only inspired them by the way he lives his life but also encouraged me as a writer and speaker as a byproduct. Who will you encourage today? Be that person that someone will call five, ten or twenty years from now and say, *"Thank you, I couldn't have done it without you!"*

3. A Legacy of Purpose - People are most energized when they are using their strengths and talents for a purpose beyond themselves. To leave a legacy of purpose, make your life about something bigger than you. While you're not going to live forever you can live on through the legacy you leave and the positive impact you make in the world. Live **on, in and with** Purpose!

4. A Legacy of Love - I often think about my grandmother, who gave to us freely even in very humble beginnings. When I think about her I don't recall her faults and mistakes. After all, who is perfect? But what I remember most about her was her love for me and my sister. She gave me a legacy of love that I now share with my children and others. Share a legacy of love and it will embrace generations to come.

Start With Your End In Mind

If you've ever read the Steven Covey book, *"The 7 Habits of Highly Effective People"*, you will find that he lists as Habit #2, "Start with the end in mind". This is perfect advice for a woman who wants to get started in her own business, because it propels her into thinking about what would be the last words anyone would have to say about her. It would bring forth questions like, *"What do I want people's last words to be about me?"*, but even more than that *"What do I want God's final word to be about me?"*

Sometimes we find ourselves achieving victories that are empty--successes that have come at the expense of things that were far less valuable. If your ladder is not leaning against the right wall, every step you take gets you to the wrong place faster.

The ability to envision in your mind what you cannot presently see with your eyes is critical to what you leave behind. The truth is, we all want to leave behind something that is bigger than ourselves and even if our end isn't exactly what the Queen of Sheba's was, we must be mindful that we are working on something to leave behind.

Many of us have children we want to leave a heritage of sorts; our families are the greatest legacy we leave. But it doesn't have to be the only thing. It is based on the principle that all things are created twice like when God formed the world in the creation. There is a mental (God said) creation, and a physical (and it was) creation. The physical creation follows the mental, just as a business follows a model. If you don't make a conscious effort to visualize who you are and what you want in life, then you empower other people and circumstances to shape you and your life by default. It's about connecting again with your own uniqueness and then defining the personal, moral, and ethical guidelines within which you can most happily express and fulfill yourself.

"Begin with the end in mind" means to begin each day, task, or project with a clear vision of your desired direction and destination, and then continue by flexing your proactive muscles to make things happen. Steven Covey made this a habit and so should every entrepreneur.

Think about and write down your own personal vision statement. It will help you focus on what you want to be and do. It is your plan for success. It is your affirmation of who you are and what your goals are in focus, and it helps to move your ideas into your reality.

Your vision statement makes you responsible and focused about your own life and purpose. With all of us, there is something much bigger we have been created to do and be in the world. If an entrepreneur is a vision given to you by God, fulfill it today. Your legacy will be there for your children, your family and the world tomorrow.

I trust that you have gained something over the course of these chapters that would lead you in moving out as an entrepreneur. The goal of the book is to release you into entrepreneurial independence and leave your footprint.

The following bonus chapters are extra motivation to get you started on the journey. The Queen of Sheba left us a beautiful legacy in the life she lived along with the seven keys I've shared with you today:

- ℘ Wisdom
- ℘ The 'C' Factor
- ℘ Principle
- ℘ Order
- ℘ Praise
- ℘ Giving
- ℘ Legacy

If you got something from this book, I'd love to hear from you. Feel free to visit me online to share your stories and testimonies at www.michellegines.com.

chapter eight

INTERESTING FACTS ABOUT SHEBA
A few things that will make you say, hmmm.

In my study of the Queen of Sheba, I was quite curious about the hard questions she asked Solomon.

Here are a few that you too might find interesting.

According to Josephus, *"upon the king's kind reception of her, he both showed a great desire to please her, and easily comprehending in his mind the meaning of the curious questions she propounded to him, he resolved them."* Not only did Sheba ask Solomon philosophical questions; she also tested him with riddles. The Targum Sheni, Midrash Mischle, and Midrash Hachefez describe one of her riddles. [xii]

"What is it? An enclosure with ten doors; when one is open, nine are shut, and when nine are open, one is shut," Sheba asked Solomon. Solomon answered, "The enclosure is the womb, and the ten doors are the ten orifices of man, namely his eyes, his ears, his nostrils, his mouth, the apertures for discharge of excreta and urine, and the navel. When the child is still in its mother's womb, the navel is open, but all the other apertures are shut, but when the child issues from the womb the navel is closed and the other orifices are open. [xiii]

In another riddle pertaining to the body, Sheba posed to Solomon, "Seven leave and nine enter; two pour out the draught and only one drinks." How did Solomon respond? "Seven are the days of woman's menstruation, nine the months of her pregnancy; her two breasts nourish the child, and one drinks." [xiv]

The Queen of Sheba propounded to Solomon the following three riddles to test his wisdom: "What is a well of wood, a pail of iron which draws up stones and pours out water?" Solomon answered, "A tube of cosmetic." [xv]

"What is that which comes from the earth as dust, the food of which is dust, which is poured out like water, and which looketh toward the house?" Solomon answered, "Naphtha." [xvi]

"What is that which precedeth all, like a general; which crieth loudly and bitterly; the head of which is like a reed; which is the glory of the rich and the shame of the poor, the glory of the dead and the shame of the living; the joy of the birds and the sorrow of the fishes?" Solomon answered, "Flax." [xvii]

"A woman saith unto her son, 'Thy father is my father, thy grandfather my husband; thou art my son; I am thy sister.'" Solomon answered, "This mother is one of the daughters of Lot, who were with child by their father" (comp. Gen. xix.). [xviii]

Arabic tradition also tells of Solomon solving riddles and of other proofs of his wisdom, and contains in general most of the stories found in Jewish tradition (Grünbaum, *l.c.*). [xix]

✖ BONUS ✖

BUSINESS TREASURE CHEST

This section is a compilation of resources, tips and tidbits to assist you in getting started and/or moving forward. The things you will find here will take the guess work out of finding where to begin. Enjoy!

chapter nine

7 TOOLS FOR ALL TRADES

1. **ONLINE RESOURCES**
- **Websites**
  - Sparkandhustle.com
  - Sba.gov
  - Entrepreneur.com
  - Ladieswholaunch.com
  - Enterprisingwomen.com (website also offers a magazine for entrepreneurial women)
  - http://womeninbusiness.about.com/
- **Blogs**
  - Sylvia Browder's blog for Women Entrepreneurs @ Sylviabrowder.com
  - The Secret of Success blog@ womenentrepreneursecrets.blogspot.com

- **Important Documents/ Entity**
  - Website: http://www.sba.gov/category/navigation-structure/starting-managing-business/managing-business/forms
    - Forms needed for managing a business

2. LEGAL RESOURCES

- Website: http://www.sba.gov/category/navigation-structure/starting-managing-business/starting-business/business-law-regulations
  - Business Laws and Regulations
    - Advertising Law
    - Employment & Labor Law
    - Finance Law
    - Intellectual Property
    - Online Business Law
    - Privacy Law
    - Environmental Regulations
    - Uniform Commercial Code
    - Contact a Government Agency
    - Workplace Safety & Health
    - Foreign Workers, Immigration, and Employee Eligibility

3. FINANCIAL RESOURCES

- Website: http://www.sba.gov/category/navigation-structure/starting-managing-business/starting-business/preparing-your-finances
  - Understanding the Basics
  - Breakeven analysis: Know when you can expect a profit

4. **TAX RESOURCES**
- Website: http://www.sba.gov/category/navigation-structure/starting-managing-business/starting-business/establishing-business/taxes
    - Getting a Tax Identification Number
    - Business Structure and Tax Implications
    - Small Business Expenses and Tax Deductions
    - Employment Taxes for Employers and Self Employed Individuals
    - Filing and Paying Your Taxes
    - Managing Your Tax Obligations
    - Learn About Your State and Local Taxes
    - Tax Help and Training
    - Tax Information for Specific Business Types
    - Fact Sheet: Tax Breaks for Small Businesses

5. **BUSINESS STARTUP RESOURCES**
- Website: http://www.sba.gov/content/templates-writing-business-plan
    - Business Plan Essentials
        - Business Plan Executive Summary
        - Market Analysis
        - Company description
        - Organization & Management
        - Marketing & Sales Management
        - Service or Product Line
        - Funding Request
        - Financial Projections
        - Marketing Plan

6. VENTURE CAPITAL RESOURCES

- Website: http://www.sba.gov/content/new-markets-venture-capital-companies
    - The New Markets Venture Capital Companies-seek to stimulate economic development in Low Income areas.
    - SBIC- The Small Business Investment Company- private, profit-seeking investment companies licensed and regulated by SBA.

7. BUSINESS WOMEN'S GROUPS & ORGANIZATIONS

- Networking
    - ABWA-American Business Women's Association
    - NAFE- National Association of Female Executives
    - NAWBO- National Association of Women Business Owners
    - National Association of Women on the Rise http://nawomenrise.com/

chapter ten

7 WAYS TO GET BETTER

1. ***The Bible is our guiding principle.*** If we stick with God in the principles, He will show up for us in the promises. Women in business must cultivate a high-standard of integrity.

2. ***Successful businesswomen are self-directed*** to seek essential knowledge, skills, and inspiration to meet their goals.

3. ***Promote enduring and cooperative relationships*** that produce high-value business networks for far-reaching positive community affiliations.

4. ***Seek service opportunities*** to bolster management skills, advance peer visibility, and improve professional marketability.

5. ***Attain comprehensive programs*** to foster business growth, sustainability, and vitality in today's dynamic market.

6. ***Promote peer fraternity and mentoring*** where accomplished women find respite from the demands of fiscal, administration, and professional responsibilities.

7. ***Celebrate and honor*** the accomplishments of outstanding businesswomen to affirm and validate our achievements, ideals, and belief systems.

chapter eleven

7 REASONS <u>YOU</u> NEED THE KEYS

1. You will come alive and dramatically **increase your enthusiasm and happiness.**

2. Your work won't feel like work, **it will feel like fun.**

3. You will get very, very clear on your **priorities in life.**

4. You will attract new, interesting, **like-minded people** in your life.

5. You will see **possibilities and opportunities** where you didn't know they existed before.

6. You will have **increased energy** and find that time just flies because you love what you do.

7. You will **no longer sweat the small stuff**, because life is exciting, fun, and passionate!

chapter twelve

7 STREAMS OF INCOME FOR YOU

1. Wholesale your product – If you only sell your product at retail, consider branching out into the world of wholesaling. Wholesaling is the sale of your goods, usually in large quantity at lower prices, to a retailer for resale purposes.

2. Retail your product – Do you currently only sell your product at wholesale? Then consider selling it at retail. You can set up your own online store quickly and easily or sell on sites like Amazon, eBay and etsy.

3. Write a book – Do you have knowledge, information or experience in a particular area that you could share with others? Then write an e-book and sell it. Not sure how to write and sell a book? Contact our team at Purpose Publishing, www.purposepublishing.com

4. Offer consulting - Share your knowledge, experience and information by consulting with people one-on-one. For example, if you're a successful graphic designer, you can teach new designers how to set up their website, price their packages, buy the software, bill clients, create a portfolio, etc.

5. Teach a class – Like consulting, teaching a class allows you to share your knowledge, experience and information with others, but on a larger scale. You can teach classes locally or offer them online using a cool Internet-based "classroom".

6. Speak – Are you great on stage? Then launch a speaking career *and* another stream of income. You can speak at conferences, trade shows and sales meetings and earn money doing it.

7. Sell newsletter subscriptions – Again, if you have knowledge, experience or information to share, you can profit from it by writing a newsletter and charging a subscription fee for it. Once you build up your subscribers, you can make a nice chunk of change from it. Last January, Chris Brogan started a weekly newsletter. He charges $9.97 per month and now has 480 subscribers. You do the math.

about the author

Michelle L. Gines

Michelle Gines is a national speaker, author and avid business woman who motivates audiences of all ages. As a mother of three, she certainly knows how to multi-task, recognize the gift and cultivate the Spirit- within herself and those around her.

God impressed upon Michelle's heart, years ago, the spirit of entrepreneurship. She's been working since she was 14; earned her first $100 selling candy to neighborhood kids at age 9 and was a vigorous sales intern for Discover Mid-America Newspaper right out of high school.

Michelle now serves as Owner/ National Administrator of her own publishing company, Purpose Publishing. In 2009, Michelle self published her first book and the Spirit of God said "You can do this yourself". With that she researched, studied and learned all she could about the publishing industry, and in 2010 Purpose Publishing was launched! God showed Michelle how to take her gifts (writing, teaching, sales, and marketing) and put them to work for herself in her business.

Michelle began her career as a sales and marketing professional with Hallmark Cards, Inc. From there, while serving as an outreach and marketing director for a local nonprofit organization, Michelle developed and delivered numerous workshops for the constituents. Encouraged by a colleague, she began to develop and deliver workshops outside of the organization, which led her further into a career as an author and speaker. Michelle has shared her presentations at schools, churches and community organizations covering topics such as self sufficiency, diversity, career management, leadership and profitable parenting. Her capstone workshop is titled, "Sandbags to Sailboats: How to Set Yourself Free for Better Living" was featured in INK Magazine in October 2010. She has recently added a new workshop entitled, "Create Your Own Cow" 10 Steps to Being an Entrepreneur".

One of Michelle's colleagues called her "pure lightning in a bottle". Michelle lights up the stage and fires up her audience. People love to talk and network with her." In fact, she does have an infectious, effervescent personality. Perhaps that's one reasons she is so well received in schools, corporations and the community.

Today, in addition to speaking and writing, Michelle reserves some of her professional time for giving back to the community as a mentor, resource development liaison and business coach. Most importantly, Michelle is a believer in the

Lord Jesus Christ and makes Him the most important part of all she does. In fact, she relies upon His strength and not her own in the work He has called her to do.

Her motto is truly, "To God be <u>all</u> Glory, Honor & Praise".

Michelle resides in Raymore, Missouri with her husband and three children. For more information or to request Michelle as a speaker for your group contact her online at:

www.michellegines.com

www.purposepublishing.com

LIKE OUR PAGE
www.facebook.com/ purposepublishing

FOLLOW US ON TWITTER
#PPublishing

REFERENCES

Books

Budge, Sir Ernest A. Wallis, translator, **The Queen Of Sheba And Her Only Son Menyelek, (The Kebra Negast)**, Oxford University Press, London, 1932

Orr, James, M.A., D.D. **General Editor. "Entry for Queen of Sheba"**. "International Standard Bible Encyclopedia". 1915.

Madden, Annette. **In Her Footsteps: 101 Remarkable Black Women from the Queen of Sheba to Queen Latifah**. Berkeley, California: Conari Press, 2000.

Rosenberg, Donna. **Instructor's Manual: World Mythology**. Lincolnwood, Illinois: NTC Publishing Group, 1986.

Time Books. **Myth and Mankind, Epics of Early Civilization: Myths of the Ancient Near East**. London: Duncan Baird Publishers, 1998.

Littmann, **The Legend of the Queen of Sheba in the Tradition of Axum**, Princeton, 1904;

Online Resources
www. Jewish Encyclopedia.com
- Ewald, Gesch. 2d ed., iii. 362-364, Göttingen, 1853;
- Grünbaum, Neue Beiträge zur Semitischen Sagenkunde, pp. 199, 211-221, Leyden, 1893;
- Grunwald, Mittheilungen der Gesellschaft für Jüdische Volkskunde, v. 10 (on the Jewish Middle Ages).

Commentaries
Matthew Henry
Holy Bible, King James Version

Reference Endnotes

[i] Budge, Sir Ernest A. Wallis, translator, **The Queen Of Sheba And Her Only Son Menyelek, (The Kebra Negast)**, Oxford University Press, London, 1932.

[ii] Budge, Sir Ernest A. Wallis, translator, **The Queen Of Sheba And Her Only Son Menyelek, (The Kebra Negast)**, Oxford University Press, London, 1932

[iii] Budge, Sir Ernest A. Wallis, translator, **The Queen Of Sheba And Her Only Son Menyelek, (The Kebra Negast)**, Oxford University Press, London, 1932

[iv] Orr, James, M.A., D.D. **General Editor. "Entry for Queen of Sheba".** "International Standard Bible Encyclopedia". 1915

[v] Budge, Sir Ernest A. Wallis, translator, **The Queen Of Sheba And Her Only Son Menyelek, (The Kebra Negast)**, Oxford University Press, London, 1932.

[vi] Budge, Sir Ernest A. Wallis, translator, **The Queen Of Sheba And Her Only Son Menyelek, (The Kebra Negast)**, Oxford University Press, London, 1932.

[vii] Budge, Sir Ernest A. Wallis, translator, **The Queen Of Sheba And Her Only Son Menyelek, (The Kebra Negast)**, Oxford University Press, London, 1932.

[viii] Budge, Sir Ernest A. Wallis, translator, **The Queen Of Sheba And Her Only Son Menyelek, (The Kebra Negast)**, Oxford University Press, London, 1932.

[ix] Budge, Sir Ernest A. Wallis, translator, **The Queen Of Sheba And Her Only Son Menyelek, (The Kebra Negast)**, Oxford University Press, London, 1932.

[x] Orr, James, M.A., D.D. **General Editor. "Entry for Queen of Sheba".** "International Standard Bible Encyclopedia". 1915

[xi] Orr, James, M.A., D.D. **General Editor. "Entry for Queen of Sheba".** "International Standard Bible Encyclopedia". 1915

[xii] www. Jewish Encyclopedia.com
Ewald, Gesch. 2d ed., iii. 362-364, Göttingen, 1853

[xiii] www. Jewish Encyclopedia.com
Ewald, Gesch. 2d ed., iii. 362-364, Göttingen, 1853

[xiv] www. Jewish Encyclopedia.com
Ewald, Gesch. 2d ed., iii. 362-364, Göttingen, 1853

[xv] www. Jewish Encyclopedia.com
Ewald, Gesch. 2d ed., iii. 362-364, Göttingen, 1853;

[xvi] Grünbaum, Neue Beiträge zur Semitischen Sagenkunde, pp. 199, 211-221, Leyden, 1893;

[xvii] Grünbaum, Neue Beiträge zur Semitischen Sagenkunde, pp. 199, 211-221, Leyden, 1893;

[xviii] Grünbaum, Neue Beiträge zur Semitischen Sagenkunde, pp. 199, 211-221, Leyden, 1893;

[xix] www. Jewish Encyclopedia.com
Grunwald, Mittheilungen der Gesellschaft für Jüdische Volkskunde, v. 10 (on the Jewish Middle Ages).

www.ingramcontent.com/pod-product-compliance
Lightning Source LLC
Chambersburg PA
CBHW052204090426
42741CB00010B/2401